LEXINGTON PUBLIC LIBRARY

 W9-CPL-064

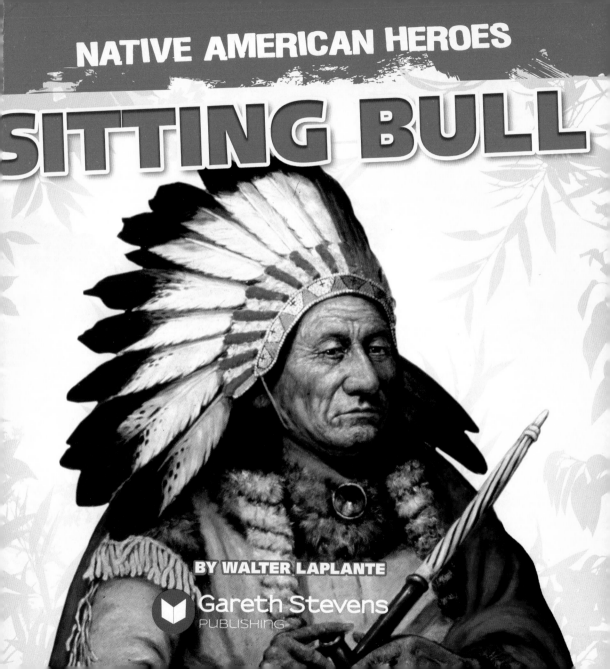

NATIVE AMERICAN HEROES

SITTING BULL

BY WALTER LAPLANTE

Gareth Stevens
PUBLISHING

Please visit our website, www.garethstevens.com. For a free color catalog of all our high-quality books, call toll free 1-800-542-2595 or fax 1-877-542-2596.

Library of Congress Cataloging-in-Publication Data

LaPlante, Walter.
Sitting Bull / Walter LaPlante.
    pages cm. — (Native American heroes)
Includes bibliographical references and index.
ISBN 978-1-4824-2700-4 (pbk.)
ISBN 978-1-4824-2701-1 (6 pack)
ISBN 978-1-4824-2702-8 (library binding)
1. Sitting Bull, 1831-1890—Juvenile literature. 2. Dakota Indians—Kings and rulers—Biography—Juvenile literature. 3. Dakota Indians—History—Juvenile literature. I. Title.
E99.D1L258 2015
978.004'9752430092—dc23
[B]
                                        2015006325

Published in 2016 by
Gareth Stevens Publishing
111 East 14th Street, Suite 349
New York, NY 10003

Copyright © 2016 Gareth Stevens Publishing

Designer: Laura Bowen
Editor: Kristen Rajczak

Photo credits: Cover, p. 1 MPI/Stringer/Archive Photos/Getty Images; cover, pp. 1–24 (series art) Binkski/Shutterstock.com; pp. 5, 19 David Francis Barry/Wikimedia Commons; p. 7 Karl Bodmer/Wikimedia Commons; p. 9 National Archives and Records Administration/Wikimedia Commons; p. 11 blinkblink/Shutterstock.com; p. 13 Hulton Archive/Stringer/Getty Images; pp. 15, 21 DEA Picture Library/De Agostini/Getty Images; p. 17 Universal History Archive/Universal Images Group/Getty Images.

All rights reserved. No part of this book may be reproduced in any form without permission in writing from the publisher, except by a reviewer.

Printed in the United States of America

CPSIA compliance information: Batch #CS15GS: For further information contact Gareth Stevens, New York, New York at 1-800-542-2595.

CONTENTS

Boldface words appear in the glossary.

Chief Sitting Bull

Sitting Bull has been honored as a Native American leader for more than a century. He led his people when their way of life was in danger. Sitting Bull's bravery and **determination** made him more than just a chief. He was a hero.

Life as a Lakota

Sitting Bull was born around 1831 to a group of Sioux (SOO) called the Lakota. They lived near the Grand River in present-day South Dakota. His name was Tatanka-Iyotanka, which means "a large buffalo at rest."

7

Sitting Bull's first battle was at age 14. He grew up to be a strong warrior and a leader in his **tribe**. He joined the Silent Eaters, a group that cared for the tribe. Around 1868, Sitting Bull became the Lakota chief.

An Unwanted Agreement

Some Sioux leaders signed a **treaty** with the US government in 1868. It said the Sioux would move to a **reservation** in South Dakota. Sitting Bull didn't sign the treaty. He also refused to bring his people to the reservation.

CANADA

UNITED STATES

Montana
Territory

Dakota Territory

Great Sioux
Reservation, 1868

Wyoming
Territory

Nebraska

Colorado
Territory

Kansas

In 1874, the US government violated, or broke, the treaty. Soon, all Sioux were told to live on the reservation, not just those who had signed the treaty. Sitting Bull gathered the Lakota as well as the Cheyenne and some Arapaho and continued to refuse.

Fighting Back

Sitting Bull had a **vision** of his people winning a great battle. It came true on June 25, 1876. US troops **attacked** Sitting Bull's camp on the Little Bighorn River in Montana Territory. They were all killed by Sitting Bull's warriors.

15

Into Hiding

After the battle, Sitting Bull was wanted by the US Army. In May 1877, he led a big group into Canada for safety. They lived there for 4 years. However, they didn't have enough food. Sitting Bull **surrendered** in 1881.

Sitting Bull was a prisoner for 2 years. He was then allowed to settle on the Sioux reservation. In 1885, Sitting Bull traveled with a wild west show. He didn't like working with the white crowds and returned home after about 4 months.

Last Moments

By 1890, a group of Native Americans loudly stated that a god would come and give them back their way of life. The US government didn't want Sitting Bull taking part in an **uprising**. He was shot while being arrested.

THE LIFE OF SITTING BULL

around 1831 ○ Sitting Bull is born.

around 1868 ○ Sitting Bull becomes the Lakota chief.

Some Sioux leaders sign the Treaty of Fort Laramie.

1874 ○ The United States violates the treaty.

1876 ○ The Battle of the Little Bighorn occurs on June 25.

1877 ○ Sitting Bull escapes to Canada.

1881 ○ Sitting Bull surrenders.

1890 ○ Sitting Bull is shot and dies.

GLOSSARY

attack: to try to harm someone or something

determination: the act of deciding something firmly

reservation: land set aside by the US government for Native Americans

surrender: to give up

treaty: an agreement between groups or countries

tribe: a group of people who live, work, and move about together

uprising: a fight against a government

vision: something seen by a way other than normal sight, such as in sleep or the imagination

FOR MORE INFORMATION

BOOKS

DiPrimio, Pete. *The Sioux of the Great Northern Plains.* Kennett Square, PA: Purple Toad Publishing, Inc., 2013.

Nelson, S. D. *Sitting Bull: Lakota Warrior and Defender of His People.* New York, NY: Abrams Books for Young Readers, 2015.

WEBSITES

Little Bighorn Battlefield
montanakids.com/history_and_prehistory/battlefields/ little_bighorn.htm
Read more about the Battle of the Little Bighorn and the national monument there today.

Native Americans: Sioux Nation
www.ducksters.com/history/native_american_sioux_ nation.php
Learn more about Sitting Bull's people, the Sioux.

Publisher's note to educators and parents: Our editors have carefully reviewed these websites to ensure that they are suitable for students. Many websites change frequently, however, and we cannot guarantee that a site's future contents will continue to meet our high standards of quality and educational value. Be advised that students should be closely supervised whenever they access the Internet.

INDEX